BOB DYLAN THE LYRICS 1961-

KNOCKIN' ON
HEAVEN'S DOOR
敲天堂的门

鲍勃·迪伦诗歌集 1961—2020
VOL.05

[美] 鲍勃·迪伦 著 李皖 译

中信出版集团 | 北京

自画像
SELF PORTRAIT

活在忧郁中 7
行吟少年 11

新晨
NEW MORNING

若非因为你 21
蝗虫之日 25
时间过得很慢 29
去见那个吉卜赛人 31
温特露德 35
如果狗儿自由奔跑 39
新晨 43
窗上的标牌 47
再过一个周末 49
我内心里的男人 53
三个天使 55
夜晚的父 57

---附加歌词---

时刻都想拥有你 59
望着河水流淌 63
当我画出我的杰作 67

目录

| 壁花 | 71 |
| 乔治·杰克逊 | 73 |

帕特·加勒特和比利小子
PAT GARRETT & BILLY THE KID

| 比利 | 83 |
| 敲天堂的门 | 89 |

CONTENTS

SELF PORTRAIT
自画像

活在忧郁中
行吟少年

> Now
> there & I am waiting / to find out the price
> you got to pay to get out of ~~doing~~ going thru everything twice
>
> Asking some little french girl with his pointed shoes & bell if she knows me very well
>
> Oh Mama / this could be the end
> (stuck) in Mobile with —
> stuck in

1969年4月24日,《纳什维尔天际线》发行3周后,迪伦再次走进录音室,开始录制自己的第10张录音室专辑,也是他第2张双唱片专辑。1970年6月8日,《自画像》发行,听众们一片错愕。

专辑收录了16首翻唱,8首迪伦原创歌曲和器乐曲(有2首是旧作的演唱会版本)。大部分歌曲都用《纳什维尔天际线》的乡村抒情嗓音演唱,也有些像是模仿"猫王"或弗兰克·西纳特拉(Frank Sinatra)。乐评人几乎是一边倒地给予了极差评价。

罗伯特·克里斯戈说:"我认识的人中间,没有一个听完了整张专辑,就算是迪伦的死忠分子也一样。我自己则是一点儿都没听。"《唱片世界》讥讽道:"变革已然结束,迪伦为琼斯先生吟唱《蓝月》。"迪伦作品最深刻的阐释者、音乐史学家格雷尔·马库斯(Greil Marcus)在评论中罕见地以这样的刻薄话开场:"这是什么狗屁玩意儿?"

迪伦把《自画像》当作一个玩笑,以撕掉评论家给他贴上的"一代人的代言人"标签。专辑的制作水平,据他说,低于他为自己设定的、在整个20世纪60年代的标准。

1984年,在时过境迁之后,迪伦接受采访时说:

"……歌迷们已经将麦克杜格尔街围得水泄不通了。我的住所外面挤满了人。我心里暗道：'好吧，去他的。我希望这些人能忘记我。我想做一些他们不可能喜欢，无法产生共鸣的事情。他们看到、听到后会说，'好吧，让我们继续找下一个人。他没什么说的了。他没有把我们想要的给我们'，你明白吧？他们会去找其他人。"

话虽如此，这张专辑仍是严肃作品，哪怕是迪伦想要自毁。录音一直严肃认真，录了差不多一年。第一阶段，1969年4月24、26日，5月3日，在纳什维尔录了3场；第二阶段，1970年3月3、5日，在纽约录了2场；第三阶段，1970年3月11日至4月3日，在纳什维尔进行了叠录。

这是迪伦在录制上最为复杂的专辑之一。只看乐手阵营黑压压一大片，简直理不出个头绪。既有《纳什维尔天际线》的原有班底，也有迪伦在20世纪60年代创作井喷期的重要合作者阿尔·库珀（Al Kooper），还包括一个16人的合唱团，甚至录音师都有4名，其中一名是迈尔斯·戴维斯的录音师。

专辑完成时正巧有个朋友有现成的颜料和画布，迪伦蘸着颜料，在画布上唰唰几笔，5分钟就完成了专辑封面油画——一个有着夏加尔风格的长脸男子简笔像。"好吧，"迪伦说，"这张专辑的名字就叫《自画像》吧。"

这么一个大杂烩，加上这么一张面孔，它的名字叫《自画像》。迪伦的意思是：来吧，看吧，这下你搞不清楚这人长啥样了吧？用他自己的话说："这是一张'我自己的盗版唱片'，它现在将终结'人们认为我是谁'的废话。"

与评论界的批评态度相反，这张专辑受到了普通听众的欢迎，专辑位列美国排行榜第4，在英国则荣登榜首。

吊诡的是，当迪伦把自己隐藏起来，让别人找不到他时，迪伦自己也找不到自己，他真的迷失了。《自画像》是迪伦人生的低潮，显而易见。

就在这张专辑发行前不久，披头士乐队解散，20世纪60年代宣告终结。而《自画像》专辑，暗示了"20世纪60年代迪伦"的终结。

但对于一个人的生命而言，低潮和失败都是其组成部分，甚至是不可缺少的部分。对于有"诗史"意义的迪伦来说，每一块砖都不可缺少。抽掉了任意一块，这个"诗史"都不完整，都不可能说通。迪伦作品没有真正差的，他从没有真正缺少意义的专辑。

比如，让我们来看看《自画像》开篇，被迪伦删去，没有入选《诗歌集》、只有一句歌词的《所有疲惫的马儿》("All the Tired Horses")，对这一刻的迪伦表现得多么传神！对1970年的文化史，又是多么明晰的时代印记："烈日下所有疲惫的马儿/我要怎样才能骑得上去啊？"（All the tired horses in the sun / How'm I s'posed to get any ridin' done?）英国文学批评家克里斯托弗·里克斯在《罪之瞳》一书中解释道，《牛津英语词典》对"在阳光下"（in the sun）的第一条释义，就是"不再忧虑或悲伤"。

LIVING THE BLUES

Since you've been gone
I've been walking around
With my head bowed down to my shoes
I've been living the blues
Ev'ry night without you

I don't have to go far
To know where you are
Strangers all give me the news
I've been living the blues
Ev'ry night without you

I think that it's best
I soon get some rest
And forget my pride
But I can't deny
This feeling that I
Carry for you deep down inside

If you see me this way
You'd come back and you'd stay
Oh, how could you refuse

活在忧郁中

自你离开后
我一直走来走去
脑袋耷拉到鞋尖
我活在忧郁中
在每一个没有你的夜晚

我不用走远
就知道你在哪儿
陌生人都给了我消息
我活在忧郁中
在每一个没有你的夜晚

我想这样最好
我很快得到了休息
也忘掉自己的尊严
可是我无法戒掉
内心深处
对你的情感

如果你能看见我这样
你就会回来,就会留下
啊,你怎么能拒绝呢

I've been living the blues
Ev'ry night without you

我活在忧郁中
在每一个没有你的夜晚

MINSTREL BOY

Who's gonna throw that minstrel boy a coin?
Who's gonna let it roll?
Who's gonna throw that minstrel boy a coin?
Who's gonna let it down easy to save his soul?

Oh, Lucky's been drivin' a long, long time
And now he's stuck on top of the hill
With twelve forward gears, it's been a long hard climb
And with all of them ladies, though, he's lonely still

Who's gonna throw that minstrel boy a coin?
Who's gonna let it roll?
Who's gonna throw that minstrel boy a coin?
Who's gonna let it down easy to save his soul?

Well, he deep in number and heavy in toil
Mighty Mockingbird, he still has such a heavy load
Beneath his bound'ries, what more can I tell
With all of his trav'lin', but I'm still on that road

行吟少年

谁会给行吟少年扔一枚钢镚儿?
谁会让它翻滚?
谁会给行吟少年扔一枚钢镚儿?
谁会让它轻轻落下拯救少年的灵魂?

啊,幸运儿[1]已开了很久很久
如今他卡在了山顶
用十二个前进挡,这是漫长艰苦的攀登
然而他还是孤独,尽管身边有这么多女人

谁会给行吟少年扔一枚钢镚儿?
谁会让它翻滚?
谁会给行吟少年扔一枚钢镚儿?
谁会让它轻轻落下拯救少年的灵魂?

唉,他深陷于数字,疲于奔命
巨大的嘲笑鸟,他的背负仍如此沉重
在他的底线下,对于他的旅程
我还能说什么呢,而我仍然在那途中

---

[1] 幸运儿,汽车名,音译为勒基。

Who's gonna throw that minstrel boy a coin?
Who's gonna let it roll?
Who's gonna throw that minstrel boy a coin?
Who's gonna let it down easy to save his soul?

谁会给行吟少年扔一枚钢镚儿?
谁会让它翻滚?
谁会给行吟少年扔一枚钢镚儿?
谁会让它轻轻落下拯救少年的灵魂?

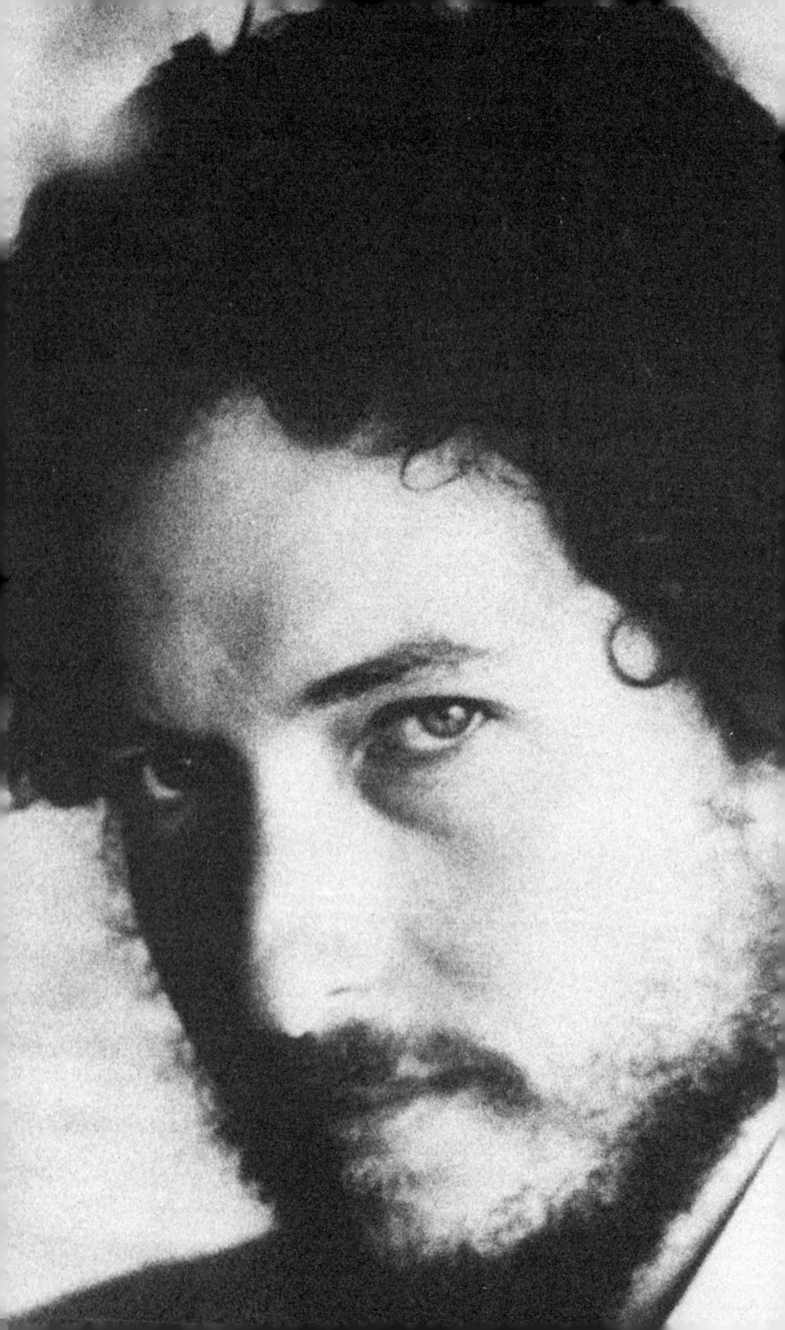

NEW MORNING
新晨

若非因为你

蝗虫之日

时间过得很慢

去见那个吉卜赛人

温特露德

如果狗儿自由奔跑

新晨

窗上的标牌

再过一个周末

我内心里的男人

三个天使

夜晚的父

附加歌词

时刻都想拥有你 壁花
望着河水流淌 乔治·杰克逊
当我画出我的杰作

BIRD ON THE HORIZON, SITTING ON A FENCE
He's singing his song for me at his own expence
And I'm just like that Bird
Oh singing just for you
I hope that you can hear
HEAR ME singing thru these tears

《新晨》确实像是新生。一个人经历过黑暗，经历过生命的低潮，经历过崩溃——他度过了，灵魂又醒过来了。世界重新发出了动人的光亮，一切又焕发出了意义。

迪伦这第11张录音室专辑，在恶评如潮的《自画像》发布仅4个月后，即由哥伦比亚唱片公司于1970年10月21日发行。让人不由得怀疑，迪伦是急于还击，要洗掉身上的"狗屎"，对外界的严厉批评立即做出回应。

但是，在《自画像》还未发行时，《新晨》已经在推进了。录音室的档案可证，当《自画像》于1970年6月8日正式发行时，《新晨》的大部分内容已经完成。

专辑录制起始于1970年5月1日。加上6月1日至5日，6月30日，7月13、23日，8月12日，总计进行了10场录音，录制了50余首歌曲。主录音地点移至纽约，告别了之前连录4张专辑的纳什维尔。

是年春天，迪伦参与了美国桂冠诗人阿奇博尔德·麦克利什（Archibald MacLeish）的新戏剧——《魔鬼》（Scratch）的制作。麦克利什邀请迪伦写几首歌，因此，双方多次见面和交流。迪伦在自传《编年史》（第一卷）中，讲述了麦克利什给他的触动。"这部戏剧调子阴暗，描绘了一个充满偏执、黑恶和恐惧的世界——它完全不见天日，直面原子时代，散发出劣行的臭气。"他对为该戏剧写歌没有信心。

不久，迪伦与该剧制作人发生冲突，退出了剧组，撤回为该剧写作的《新晨》《时间过得很慢》和《夜晚的父》。《新晨》联合制作人阿尔·库珀认为，这3首歌几乎是专辑的支点，让迪伦写了更多东西。

的确，专辑中的多首歌曲有一种与迪伦其他专辑都不同的气质，像是具有某种宗教性的肃穆。这种影响可能来自麦克利什。在最后一次会面时，迪伦这样写道："我们中间的大多数人几乎没有离开过地面，他却已经到了月球。在某种程度上，他教会我如何游过大西洋。我想谢谢他，却发现很难开口。我们在路边挥手告别，我知道我再也不会见到他了。"

《新晨》将舆论反转过来，受到了歌迷和评论家的热烈欢迎。

从音乐角度看，《新晨》回归了民谣摇滚。迪伦以大量的原声吉他、偶露峥嵘的钢琴演奏、锦上添花的管风琴，以及3名合唱人员带来的黑人福音颂歌，歌唱了大地、爱情、宁静生活和蕴含其中的一种精神。

这张专辑寻常中又有不寻常。表面上，许多歌都很简单，描绘乡村生活中琐碎的快乐：小溪里捉鱼，厨房里看星星，听公鸡打鸣，看野兔过马路，看土拨鼠沿溪流奔跑，开车行驶过乡村公路，和妻子、孩子一起钓彩虹鱼……但平凡事物表面，都有一种光辉，像是寂静的永恒（歌曲《新晨》《时间过得很慢》《窗上的标牌》）。你也很难想象，

《如果狗儿自由奔跑》能成为一首宏伟的交响曲，仿佛是宇宙的赞歌。圣诞节早晨对来自高处的天使的感知，建立在毫无意义甚至疲惫、冷酷的城市街景之上，混凝土的世界遍布着灵魂（歌曲《三个天使》）。此外就是情歌，如《若非因为你》《温特露德》《再过一个周末》《我内心里的男人》。令人意外的是，它们都是恩爱夫妻的简单赞歌，庆祝自然和感官的简单乐趣，除此之外并无其他。最后，终曲《夜晚的父》，仰望上空，彻底越过了尘世，注目于琐碎日常之上至高大的存在。《新晨》专辑给人一种包豪斯主义极简建筑的感觉，即使你对某首具体的歌曲有意见，也不可以抽掉它，歌曲之间有一种相辅相成、相反相成、相互支撑的力。

《新晨》专辑也受到了一些批评。其中最主要的意见，若在中国文化语境中表述，就是：迪伦世界观的终点，不过是"老婆孩子热炕头"。"新晨"更像是一个虚假的黎明，它的主题不过是流行歌曲的主题。

我觉得，这个议论似是而非，区别即在于那种光亮。生活是不能否定的。人生的意义最终就是它本身。迪伦在这里是完全不外求的，"除了生活自身的美，没有任何信息"，对此他非常自觉，"这一定就是全部的意义"（歌曲《窗上的标牌》）。可能迪伦的错误，如果说真错了的话，就是他无视人间的疾苦和不公正，直接抵达了这个结论。

IF NOT FOR YOU

If not for you
Babe, I couldn't find the door
Couldn't even see the floor
I'd be sad and blue
If not for you

If not for you
Babe, I'd lay awake all night
Wait for the mornin' light
To shine in through
But it would not be new
If not for you

If not for you
My sky would fall
Rain would gather too
Without your love I'd be nowhere at all
I'd be lost if not for you
And you know it's true

If not for you
My sky would fall

若非因为你

若非因为你
宝贝,我会摸不到门
甚至也看不见地
我会悲伤又忧郁
若非因为你

若非因为你
宝贝,我会彻夜不眠
等着那清晨的光
照彻房间
但它也不会是新的
若非因为你

若非因为你
我的天会塌
雨也会聚集
没有你的爱我无处可去
我会迷失,若非因为你
你知道这都是真的

若非因为你
我的天会塌

Rain would gather too
Without your love I'd be nowhere at all
Oh! what would I do
If not for you

If not for you
Winter would have no spring
Couldn't hear the robin sing
I just wouldn't have a clue
Anyway it wouldn't ring true
If not for you

雨也会聚集
没有你的爱我无处可去
啊！我能怎么办呢
若非因为你

若非因为你
冬不会有春
听不到知更鸟歌吟
我会茫然了无头绪
反正这听起来极不真实
若非因为你

DAY OF THE LOCUSTS

Oh, the benches were stained with tears and perspiration
The birdies were flying from tree to tree
There was little to say, there was no conversation
As I stepped to the stage to pick up my degree
And the locusts sang off in the distance
Yeah, the locusts sang such a sweet melody
Oh, the locusts sang off in the distance
Yeah, the locusts sang and they were singing for me

I glanced into the chamber where the judges were talking
Darkness was everywhere, it smelled like a tomb
I was ready to leave, I was already walkin'
But the next time I looked there was light in the room
And the locusts sang, yeah, it give me a chill
Oh, the locusts sang such a sweet melody
Oh, the locusts sang their high whining trill
Yeah, the locusts sang and they were singing for me

蝗虫之日 [1]

啊,长椅上沾染了泪水和汗水
小鸟从一树飞向另一树
无话可说,没有对话
当我走上台领取学位证书
蝗虫在远方唱着
是啊,蝗虫唱出了如此甜美的旋律
啊,蝗虫在远方唱着
是啊,蝗虫在唱,它们在为我而歌吟

我瞥了一眼会议厅,评审人正在交谈
到处都是黑暗,闻起来像座坟茔
我准备离开,我已经迈步
但这一次我看到,房间里有光亮
而蝗虫在唱,是的,歌声让我阵阵发冷
啊,蝗虫唱出了如此甜美的旋律
啊,蝗虫唱着高高的哀泣的颤音
是啊,蝗虫在唱,它们在为我而歌吟

---

[1] 1970年6月9日,迪伦被普林斯顿大学授予荣誉博士学位。这首歌描述了他经历此事的感受。在自传中他描述道:"那是一次古怪的冒险之旅……我站在热浪里,瞪视着人群,做着白日梦,不断地分心走神。"歌名援引了美国作家纳撒尼尔·韦斯特的小说名。本篇由杨盈盈校译。

Outside of the gates the trucks were unloadin'
The weather was hot, a-nearly 90 degrees
The man standin' next to me, his head was exploding
Well, I was prayin' the pieces wouldn't fall on me
Yeah, the locusts sang off in the distance
Yeah, the locusts sang such a sweet melody
Oh, the locusts sang off in the distance
And the locusts sang and they were singing for me

I put down my robe, picked up my diploma
Took hold of my sweetheart and away we did drive
Straight for the hills, the black hills of Dakota
Sure was glad to get out of there alive
And the locusts sang, well, it give me a chill
Yeah, the locusts sang such a sweet melody
And the locusts sang with a high whinin' trill
Yeah, the locusts sang and they was singing for me
Singing for me, well, singing for me

一重重大门外,卡车在卸货
天气炎热,差不多90度[1]
站我旁边的人,他的脑袋正在爆炸
好吧,我在祈祷碎片不会落在我身上
是啊,蝗虫在远方唱着
是啊,蝗虫唱出了如此甜美的旋律
啊,蝗虫在远方唱着
蝗虫在唱,它们在为我而歌吟

我脱下了黑袍,拿起我的证书
相拥着心上人,我们驱车离去
直奔着那群山,达科他的黑色山岭
确实开心啊,活着离开了那里
而蝗虫在唱,唉,歌声让我阵阵发冷
是啊,蝗虫唱出了如此甜美的旋律
蝗虫唱着高高的哀泣的颤音
是啊,蝗虫在唱,它在为我而歌吟
为我而歌吟,唉,为我而歌吟

---

[1] 此处指90华氏度,约为32摄氏度。

TIME PASSES SLOWLY

Time passes slowly up here in the mountains
We sit beside bridges and walk beside fountains
Catch the wild fishes that float through the stream
Time passes slowly when you're lost in a dream

Once I had a sweetheart, she was fine and good-lookin'
We sat in her kitchen while her mama was cookin'
Stared out the window to the stars high above
Time passes slowly when you're searchin' for love

Ain't no reason to go in a wagon to town
Ain't no reason to go to the fair
Ain't no reason to go up, ain't no reason to go down
Ain't no reason to go anywhere

Time passes slowly up here in the daylight
We stare straight ahead and try so hard to stay right
Like the red rose of summer that blooms in the day
Time passes slowly and fades away

时间过得很慢

这山中的时间过得很慢
我们在桥畔闲坐,在喷泉边漫步
捕捉溪水中漂来漂去的野鱼
时间过得很慢,当你迷失在梦中

我曾有个心上人,她娇小又貌美
她妈妈做饭时,我们就坐在厨房里
注视着窗外高高在上的星星
时间过得很慢,当你找寻着爱情

没理由乘马车进城
没理由去集市
没理由登高,没理由下山
没理由去哪里

这儿的白天,时间过得很慢
我们直视着前方,努力不使之偏向
就像夏日的红玫瑰在白昼绽放
时间过得很慢,渐渐消隐无踪

WENT TO SEE THE GYPSY

Went to see the gypsy
Stayin' in a big hotel
He smiled when he saw me coming
And he said, "Well, well, well"
His room was dark and crowded
Lights were low and dim
"How are you?" he said to me
I said it back to him

I went down to the lobby
To make a small call out
A pretty dancing girl was there
And she began to shout
"Go on back to see the gypsy
He can move you from the rear
Drive you from your fear
Bring you through the mirror
He did it in Las Vegas
And he can do it here"

去见那个吉卜赛人

去见那个吉卜赛人 [1]
在他下榻的大酒店
看见我来他笑了
然后说:"哦,哦,哦"
他的房间昏黑拥挤
灯又暗又低
"你好吗?"他对我说
我也用这句话回他

我下楼到大厅
打一个简短的电话
有个漂亮舞女在那儿
她开始喊
"回去看那个吉卜赛人
他可以从后面移动你
帮你驱走恐惧
带你穿越镜子
他在拉斯维加斯做过
在这里也一样可以"

---

[1] 那个吉卜赛人,指"猫王"。

Outside the lights were shining
On the river of tears
I watched them from the distance
With music in my ears

I went back to see the gypsy
It was nearly early dawn
The gypsy's door was open wide
But the gypsy was gone
And that pretty dancing girl
She could not be found
So I watched that sun come rising
From that little Minnesota town

外面的灯照着
这一条泪水之河
我远远望着它
音乐在耳中响着

我回去见吉卜赛人
天就快亮了
吉卜赛人的门大开着
可他已经走了
而那个漂亮舞女
也不见了影踪
于是我望着太阳升起
从那个明尼苏达小城[1]

---

[1]　明尼苏达小城，指迪伦的家乡。

WINTERLUDE

Winterlude, Winterlude, oh darlin'
Winterlude by the road tonight
Tonight there will be no quarrelin'
Ev'rything is gonna be all right
Oh, I see by the angel beside me
That love has a reason to shine
You're the one I adore, come over here and give me more
Then Winterlude, this dude thinks you're fine

Winterlude, Winterlude, my little apple
Winterlude by the corn in the field
Winterlude, let's go down to the chapel
Then come back and cook up a meal
Well, come out when the skating rink glistens
By the sun, near the old crossroads sign
The snow is so cold, but our love can be bold
Winterlude, don't be rude, please be mine

Winterlude, Winterlude, my little daisy

温特露德 [1]

温特露德,温特露德,啊亲爱的
今晚公路边的温特露德
今晚将无争
万事安妥
啊,我看见身边的天使
明白爱有理由闪烁
你是我钟爱的人,请过来给我更多
然后温特露德,这帅哥觉得你真不错

温特露德,温特露德,我的小苹果
田间玉米边的温特露德
温特露德,我们去教堂吧
然后回家做饭生火
哦,等溜冰场在太阳下发光
我们再出门,就在老十字路牌附近
雪真冷啊,但我们的爱可以放亮
温特露德,别无礼,请做我的女人

温特露德,温特露德,我的小雏菊

---

[1] 迪伦用冬日(winter)和乐曲(lude)合成一个女性的名字,其发音为温特露德。

Winterlude by the telephone wire
Winterlude, it's makin' me lazy
Come on, sit by the logs in the fire
The moonlight reflects from the window
Where the snowflakes, they cover the sand
Come out tonight, ev'rything will be tight
Winterlude, this dude thinks you're grand

温特露德,你在电话线那一端
温特露德,这让我慵懒
来吧,坐到燃烧的原木边
月光映着窗子
雪花,覆盖着白沙
今晚出来吧,一切都会很妙
温特露德,这帅哥觉得你真飒

IF DOGS RUN FREE

If dogs run free, then why not we
Across the swooping plain?
My ears hear a symphony
Of two mules, trains and rain
The best is always yet to come
That's what they explain to me
Just do your thing, you'll be king
If dogs run free

If dogs run free, why not me
Across the swamp of time?
My mind weaves a symphony
And tapestry of rhyme
Oh, winds which rush my tale to thee
So it may flow and be
To each his own, it's all unknown
If dogs run free

If dogs run free, then what must be
Must be, and that is all
True love can make a blade of grass
Stand up straight and tall

如果狗儿自由奔跑

如果狗儿自由奔跑,那么我们何不去穿过
这俯冲的莽原?
我的耳朵听到
两头骡子、几列火车和雨的交响曲
最好的总是还在路上
它们这么解释给我
做好你自己的事,你就是君王
如果狗儿自由奔跑

如果狗儿自由奔跑,那么我何不去穿过
这时光的泥沼?
我的心编织了一支交响曲
和一匹韵律的织锦
啊,风把我的故事吹向你
所以它可以飘荡,成为
每个人自己的传奇,一切都是未知的
如果狗儿自由奔跑

如果狗儿自由奔跑,那么必当如此的
就当如此,就是这样
真爱可以让一片草叶
站得又高又直

In harmony with the cosmic sea

True love needs no company

It can cure the soul, it can make it whole

If dogs run free

与宇宙的海洋和谐一体
真爱不需要陪伴
它可以治愈灵魂,使其完整
如果狗儿自由奔跑

NEW MORNING

Can't you hear that rooster crowin'?
Rabbit runnin' down across the road
Underneath the bridge where the water flowed through
So happy just to see you smile
Underneath the sky of blue
On this new morning, new morning
On this new morning with you

Can't you hear that motor turnin'?
Automobile comin' into style
Comin' down the road for a country mile or two
So happy just to see you smile
Underneath the sky of blue
On this new morning, new morning
On this new morning with you

The night passed away so quickly
It always does when you're with me

Can't you feel that sun a-shinin'?
Groundhog runnin' by the country stream
This must be the day that all of my dreams come true

新晨

你听不到公鸡在叫吗?
兔子正跑过马路
桥下面,河水流动
只是看见你微笑就无比开心
在蓝色天空下
在这个新晨,新晨
和你一起在这个新晨

你听不到马达在转动吗?
汽车正开始流行
沿这条路开一两段路
只是看见你微笑就无比开心
在蓝色天空下
在这个新晨,新晨
和你一起在这个新晨

夜晚过得真快啊
你和我在一起时,总是这样

你感觉不到太阳在照耀吗?
土拨鼠在乡间溪流边奔跑
这一定是我的梦全都成真的一天

So happy just to be alive
Underneath the sky of blue
On this new morning, new morning
On this new morning with you

So happy just to be alive
Underneath the sky of blue
On this new morning, new morning
On this new morning with you
New morning . . .

只是活着,就很幸福
在蓝色天空下
在这个新晨,新晨
和你一起在这个新晨

只是活着,就很幸福
在蓝色天空下
在这个新晨,新晨
和你一起在这个新晨
新晨……

SIGN ON THE WINDOW

Sign on the window says "Lonely"
Sign on the door said "No Company Allowed"
Sign on the street says "Y' Don't Own Me"
Sign on the porch says "Three's A Crowd"
Sign on the porch says "Three's A Crowd"

Her and her boyfriend went to California
Her and her boyfriend done changed their tune
My best friend said, "Now didn' I warn ya
Brighton girls are like the moon
Brighton girls are like the moon"

Looks like a-nothing but rain . . .
Sure gonna be wet tonight on Main Street . . .
Hope that it don't sleet

Build me a cabin in Utah
Marry me a wife, catch rainbow trout
Have a bunch of kids who call me "Pa"
That must be what it's all about
That must be what it's all about

窗上的标牌

窗上的标牌写着"单身"
门上的标牌写着"陪客禁入"
街上的标牌写着"我不归你"
廊上的标牌写着"三人太挤"
廊上的标牌写着"三人太挤"

她和男友去了加州
她和男友改了腔调
我的至交说:"瞧,我不是警告过你吗
布莱顿姑娘就像月亮
布莱顿姑娘就像月亮"

看来无非就是要下雨……
今晚肯定会在大街上淋得透湿
希望别转为雨夹雪

在犹他州给我造个小木屋
为我娶个妻子,捕捉彩虹鱼
养一群孩子叫我"爸"
这一定就是全部的意义
这一定就是全部的意义

ONE MORE WEEKEND

Slippin' and slidin' like a weasel on the run
I'm lookin' good to see you, yeah, and we can have some fun
One more weekend, one more weekend with you
One more weekend, one more weekend'll do

Come on down to my ship, honey, ride on deck
We'll fly over the ocean just like you suspect
One more weekend, one more weekend with you
One more weekend, one more weekend'll do

We'll fly the night away
Hang out the whole next day
Things will be okay
You wait and see
We'll go someplace unknown
Leave all the children home
Honey, why not go alone
Just you and me

Comin' and goin' like a rabbit in the wood
I'm happy just to see you, yeah, lookin' so good
One more weekend, one more weekend with you

再过一个周末

滑呀滑,像一只逃跑的鼬鼠
很高兴见到你,是呀,我们会玩得很开心
再过一个周末,和你再过一个周末
再过一个周末,再过一个周末就好

到我的船上来,亲爱的,在甲板上撒欢
我们将飞越海洋,就像你猜想的那样
再过一个周末,和你再过一个周末
再过一个周末,再过一个周末就好

我们将夜晚放飞
第二天闲逛整日
一切都会好
你就等着瞧吧
我们会去一个谁都不知道的地方
把孩子们都留在家里
亲爱的,为什么不单独去呢
就只我和你

来来回回,就像树林里的兔子
只看见你就很开心,是呀,看起来真好呀
再过一个周末,和你再过一个周末

One more weekend, one more weekend'll do (yes, you will!)

Like a needle in a haystack, I'm gonna find you yet
You're the sweetest gone mama that this boy's ever gonna get
One more weekend, one more weekend with you
One more weekend, one more weekend'll do

再过一个周末,再过一个周末就好(是的,你会的!)

就像草垛里的一根针,我还是会把你找到
你是这小子能找到的最贴心的出走妈妈
再过一个周末,和你再过一个周末
再过一个周末,再过一个周末就好

THE MAN IN ME

The man in me will do nearly any task
And as for compensation, there's little he would ask
Take a woman like you
To get through to the man in me

Storm clouds are raging all around my door
I think to myself I might not take it anymore
Take a woman like your kind
To find the man in me

But, oh, what a wonderful feeling
Just to know that you are near
Sets my heart a-reeling
From my toes up to my ears

The man in me will hide sometimes to keep from bein' seen
But that's just because he doesn't want to turn into some machine
Took a woman like you
To get through to the man in me

我内心里的男人

我内心里的男人几乎能完成任何任务
至于酬金,他几乎不提要求
找一个像你这样的女人
来了解我内心里的男人

乌云在我门口翻腾
我在想我可能无法再忍受
找一个像你这样的女人
去找到我内心里的男人

但是,嗨,这是多美妙的感觉啊
只是知道你在身边
我的心就一片眩晕
从脚趾直到耳根

我内心里的男人有时会躲起来,不让人瞧见
但那只是因为他不想变成
   机器
找一个像你这样的女人
来了解我内心里的男人

THREE ANGELS

Three angels up above the street

Each one playing a horn

Dressed in green robes with wings that stick out

They've been there since Christmas morn

The wildest cat from Montana passes by in a flash

Then a lady in a bright orange dress

One U-Haul trailer, a truck with no wheels

The Tenth Avenue bus going west

The dogs and pigeons fly up and they flutter around

A man with a badge skips by

Three fellas crawlin' on their way back to work

Nobody stops to ask why

The bakery truck stops outside of that fence

Where the angels stand high on their poles

The driver peeks out, trying to find one face

In this concrete world full of souls

The angels play on their horns all day

The whole earth in progression seems to pass by

But does anyone hear the music they play

Does anyone even try?

三个天使

三个天使在街道上空
每个都在吹号角
身穿绿袍,张开了双翼
从圣诞节早晨就一直在那里
蒙大拿最野的猫一闪而过
然后是穿亮橙色连衣裙的女士
一辆"优豪"拖车,一辆没有轮子的卡车
第十大道的巴士西行而去
狗和鸽子飞起来,四处扑腾
戴徽章的男子从旁边溜过
三个小伙迟缓地走回去上工
没有人停下来问为什么
面包店的车停在栅栏外
天使高高站在他们的柱子上
司机向外窥探,想找到一张脸
在这遍布着灵魂的具体世界
天使整日吹着号角
整个地球似乎正在运行中从身边经过
但是有谁听见天使吹奏的音乐
有谁,真的试着听过?

FATHER OF NIGHT

Father of night, Father of day
Father, who taketh the darkness away
Father, who teacheth the bird to fly
Builder of rainbows up in the sky
Father of loneliness and pain
Father of love and Father of rain

Father of day, Father of night
Father of black, Father of white
Father, who build the mountain so high
Who shapeth the cloud up in the sky
Father of time, Father of dreams
Father, who turneth the rivers and streams

Father of grain, Father of wheat
Father of cold and Father of heat
Father of air and Father of trees
Who dwells in our hearts and our memories
Father of minutes, Father of days
Father of whom we most solemnly praise

夜晚的父

夜晚的父,昼日的父
移去黑暗的父
教授鸟飞翔的父
空中霓虹的缔造者
孤独与痛苦的父
爱的父和雨的父

昼日的父,夜晚的父
黑的父,白的父
立起巍巍高山的父
在天上塑造出云朵
时间的父,梦境的父
使河溪百折千回的父

谷物的父,小麦的父
寒的父与暑的父
空气的父与草木的父
栖居于我们的心与我们的记忆
分秒的父,岁月的父
我们最庄严颂赞的父

I'D HAVE YOU ANY TIME
(WITH GEORGE HARRISON)

Let me in here, I know I've been here

Let me into your heart

Let me know you, let me show you

Let me roll it to you

All I have is yours

All you see is mine

And I'm glad to have you in my arms

I'd have you any time

Let me say it, let me play it

Let me lay it on you

Let me know you, let me show you

Let me grow it on you

All I have is yours

All you see is mine

And I'm glad to have you in my arms

I'd have you any time

Let me in here, I know I've been here

Let me into your heart

Let me know you, let me show you

时刻都想拥有你

（与乔治·哈里森合作）

让我进去吧，我知道我已经在这儿
就让我住进你心里
让我了解你，让我表现给你
让我为你翻来覆去
我所有的一切都是你的
你所见的一切都是我的
有你在怀真高兴啊
时刻都想拥有你

让我说出来，让我做出来
让我在你身上试一试
让我了解你，让我表现给你
让我把它种你心里
我所有的一切都是你的
你所见的一切都是我的
有你在怀真高兴啊
时刻都想拥有你

让我进去吧，我知道我已经在这儿
就让我住进你心里
让我了解你，让我表现给你

Let me roll it to you

All I have is yours

All you see is mine

And I'm glad to have you in my arms

I'd have you any time

让我为你翻来覆去
我所有的一切都是你的
你所见的一切都是我的
有你在怀真高兴啊
时刻都想拥有你

WATCHING THE RIVER FLOW

What's the matter with me
I don't have much to say
Daylight sneakin' through the window
And I'm still in this all-night café
Walkin' to and fro beneath the moon
Out to where the trucks are rollin' slow
To sit down on this bank of sand
And watch the river flow

Wish I was back in the city
Instead of this old bank of sand
With the sun beating down over the chimney tops
And the one I love so close at hand
If I had wings and I could fly
I know where I would go
But right now I'll just sit here so contentedly
And watch the river flow

People disagreeing on all just about everything, yeah
Makes you stop and all wonder why

望着河水流淌 [1]

我这是怎么了
我没有什么好说
天光悄悄潜入了窗子
可我还在这通宵咖啡馆里
在月光下踯躅
走出去到卡车缓慢驶过的地方
在这沙堤坐下来
望河水流淌

真希望我是回到了城里
而不是在这老沙堤上
阳光打在烟囱顶
所爱的人就在近旁
如果我有翅膀能飞
我知道我要飞哪儿去
但是此刻,我只心满意足坐在这儿
望河水流淌

是啊,人们对每件事都众说纷纭
让你停下来寻思,这都是为什么

---

[1] 本篇由杨盈盈校译。

Why only yesterday I saw somebody on the street
Who just couldn't help but cry
Oh, this ol' river keeps on rollin', though
No matter what gets in the way and which way the wind does blow
And as long as it does I'll just sit here
And watch the river flow

People disagreeing everywhere you look
Makes you wanna stop and read a book
Why only yesterday I saw somebody on the street
That was really shook
But this ol' river keeps on rollin', though
No matter what gets in the way and which way the wind does blow
And as long as it does I'll just sit here
And watch the river flow

Watch the river flow
Watchin' the river flow
Watchin' the river flow
But I'll sit down on this bank of sand
And watch the river flow

为什么就在昨天我还看见
有人在街上忍不住哭呢
啊,可是,这古老的河还是一直翻滚
不在乎有什么挡道,风又吹向
　何方
只要它还是这样,我就会坐这儿
望河水流淌

你瞧,到处都可见人们众说纷纭
让你想停下来,读读书
为什么就在昨天我还看见
有人在街上真的被惊吓了呢
可是,这古老的河还是一直翻滚
不在乎有什么挡道,风又吹向
　何方
只要它还是这样,我就会坐这儿
望河水流淌

望河水流淌
望着河水流淌
望着河水流淌
但是我会在这沙堤坐下来
望河水流淌

WHEN I PAINT MY MASTERPIECE

Oh, the streets of Rome are filled with rubble
Ancient footprints are everywhere
You can almost think that you're seein' double
On a cold, dark night on the Spanish Stairs
Got to hurry on back to my hotel room
Where I've got me a date with Botticelli's niece
She promised that she'd be right there with me
When I paint my masterpiece

Oh, the hours I've spent inside the Coliseum
Dodging lions and wastin' time
Oh, those mighty kings of the jungle, I could hardly stand to see 'em
Yes, it sure has been a long, hard climb
Train wheels runnin' through the back of my memory
When I ran on the hilltop following a pack of wild geese
Someday, everything is gonna be smooth like a rhapsody
When I paint my masterpiece

当我画出我的杰作

哦,罗马的街道遍地瓦砾
到处都是古人的足迹
几乎让人以为看到了重影
寒冷、黑暗的夜,在西班牙台阶[1]
我心想得快点回酒店
以便和波提切利[2]的侄女会面
她答应将在那儿陪我
当我画出我的杰作

哦,我在斗兽场度过的时辰
躲避着狮子,虚掷着时光
哦,威猛的丛林之王,它的样子我不忍
　直视
是的,这确乎是一段漫长、艰难的攀登
当我跟着一群野鹅跑上山顶
火车车轮从我记忆深处碾过
终有一天,一切都会像狂想曲般酣畅
当我画出我的杰作

---

[1] 西班牙台阶,罗马著名景点,人们常在这里相约见面。
[2] 波提切利(1445—1510),著名意大利画家,代表作有《维纳斯的诞生》。

Sailin' round the world in a dirty gondola
Oh, to be back in the land of Coca-Cola!

I left Rome and landed in Brussels
On a plane ride so bumpy that I almost cried
Clergymen in uniform and young girls pullin' muscles
Everyone was there to greet me when I stepped inside
Newspapermen eating candy
Had to be held down by big police
Someday, everything is gonna be diff'rent
When I paint my masterpiece

乘一艘脏兮兮的贡多拉[1]环游世界
哦,回到那可口可乐的国度!

我离开了罗马,在布鲁塞尔降落
飞机如此颠簸,我差点儿叫出声
穿制服的牧师和伸展肌肉的姑娘
当我走进去,所有人都在那儿相迎
报社记者嚼着糖
不得不忍受着警察大人的压制
终有一天,一切将为之一变
当我画出我的杰作

---

[1] 贡多拉,一种单人摇橹的小船,威尼斯人代步的工具。

WALLFLOWER

Wallflower, wallflower
Won't you dance with me?
I'm sad and lonely too
Wallflower, wallflower
Won't you dance with me?
I'm fallin' in love with you

Just like you I'm wondrin' what I'm doin' here
Just like you I'm wondrin' what's goin' on

Wallflower, wallflower
Won't you dance with me?
The night will soon be gone

I have seen you standing in the smoky haze
And I know that you're gonna be mine one of these days
Mine alone

Wallflower, wallflower
Take a chance on me
Please let me ride you home

壁花 [1]

壁花,壁花
你不和我跳舞吗?
我也很伤心落寞
壁花,壁花
你不和我跳舞吗?
我正落入你的爱河

就像你一样,我也不知道我在这儿干吗
就像你一样,我也想知道发生了什么

壁花,壁花
你不和我跳舞吗?
夜晚转眼就要过去

我看见你站在烟雾中
我知道有一天你会属于我
只属于我

壁花,壁花
给我个机会吧
请让我开车送你回家

---

[1] 壁花,在社交场合因害羞而没有舞伴或不与人交谈的人。

GEORGE JACKSON

I woke up this mornin'
There were tears in my bed
They killed a man I really loved
Shot him through the head
Lord, Lord
They cut George Jackson down
Lord, Lord
They laid him in the ground

Sent him off to prison
For a seventy-dollar robbery
Closed the door behind him
And they threw away the key
Lord, Lord
They cut George Jackson down
Lord, Lord
They laid him in the ground

He wouldn't take shit from no one

乔治·杰克逊 [1]

今早我醒来
床上有泪水
他们杀了我深爱的人
子弹射穿他的头颅
主,主啊
他们杀了乔治·杰克逊
主,主啊
他们将他埋入地下

为了七十美元的抢劫
他们把他送进监狱
在身后关上门
扔掉了钥匙
主,主啊
他们杀了乔治·杰克逊
主,主啊
他们将他埋入地下

他不认任何人的狗屎

---

[1] 乔治·杰克逊(1941—1971),美国黑豹党成员,1971年8月21日在美国加州圣昆汀监狱因越狱被警察枪杀。

He wouldn't bow down or kneel
Authorities, they hated him
Because he was just too real
Lord, Lord
They cut George Jackson down
Lord, Lord
They laid him in the ground

Prison guards, they cursed him
As they watched him from above
But they were frightened of his power
They were scared of his love
Lord, Lord
So they cut George Jackson down
Lord, Lord
They laid him in the ground

Sometimes I think this whole world
Is one big prison yard
Some of us are prisoners
The rest of us are guards
Lord, Lord
They cut George Jackson down
Lord, Lord
They laid him in the ground

不会低头和下跪
当权者恨他
因为他太真实
主，主啊
他们杀了乔治·杰克逊
主，主啊
他们将他埋入地下

监狱看守从上面监视他时
他们诅咒他
但他们畏惧他的力量
他们为他的爱感到害怕
主，主啊
所以他们杀了乔治·杰克逊
主，主啊
他们将他埋入地下

有时我觉得这整个世界
就是一个监狱大院
我们当中有些人是囚徒
其他人都是看守
主，主啊
他们杀了乔治·杰克逊
主，主啊
他们将他埋入地下

Bob Dylan/Soundtrack

PAT GARRETT & BILLY THE KID

PAT GARRETT & BILLY THE KID
帕特·加勒特和比利小子

比利

敲天堂的门

① Climbed upon the bell tower to gaze around at the terrain ②
I couldn't find you anywhere, you were gone like
a northern train

《帕特·加勒特和比利小子》是同名电影原声带，也是迪伦的第12张录音室专辑，由哥伦比亚唱片公司于1973年7月13日发行。

该电影的编剧鲁迪·沃利策（Rudy Wurlitzer）和饰演比利小子的主演克里斯·克里斯托弗森都是迪伦的朋友。在他们俩力荐下，迪伦不仅为电影配乐，还在片中饰演了一个小角色，牛仔阿里亚斯。

比利小子是美国南方边疆的传奇人物，一个法外之徒和神枪手。影片讲述他的好友帕特·加勒特靠出卖比利当上了新墨西哥州警长。他试图说服比利自首。比利拒绝了，遭到了逮捕。在处决他的那天，比利成功越狱脱逃。加勒特奉州长之命展开追捕。在萨姆纳堡，比利自愿死在加勒特枪下，没有反抗。

最早力荐迪伦的是克里斯托弗森。那天，迪伦到沃利策的公寓来找他，说自己已经和比利小子绑在一起了，几乎就是比利小子的转世。沃利策随即修改剧本，加入迪伦饰演的角色，然后带着他飞赴墨西哥，面见该片导演萨姆·佩金帕（Sam Peckinpah）。佩金帕原本已属意乡村歌手罗杰·米勒（Roger Miller）做配乐，并不知道迪伦要参与。见到迪伦后，他愣了好大一会儿，才缓缓说："我本人是罗杰·米勒的超级粉丝。"

迪伦第一次试奏《比利》主题曲，是在导演佩金帕的屋子里，导演旁边放着一瓶墨西哥龙舌兰酒。佩金帕说："好吧，老伙计，来看看你会什么，你带了吉他吧？"他们进了一个小房间。佩金帕有一把摇椅，迪伦就坐在摇椅前的矮凳上，演奏了三四首曲子。佩金帕出来时用手帕拭着眼睛："天哪，这小子！他到底是何方神圣？签了他！"[1]

迪伦之前没有给电影配过乐，这活儿于他而言完全陌生，他掌控不了。佩金帕的御用编曲、爵士音乐家杰里·菲尔丁（Jerry Fielding）很不接受迪伦，未承想这位摇滚巨人居然写不出一首管弦配乐。菲尔丁多次为迪伦"从不懂他想要什么"而发火。

专辑里只有2首歌——1首《比利》，共有3个版本，出现在电影的不同段落；1首《敲天堂的门》。另外6首都是器乐曲。当时大多数批评家的反应都是负面的。乔恩·兰道（Jon Landau）批评说："它和《自画像》一样无能、业余和令人尴尬，具有故意招致商业灾难的所有特征。显然它是一种调戏，（迪伦）为了将自己从观众强加给他的义务中解脱出来。"

几乎谁都没料到，《敲天堂的门》竟成了迪伦的一首世界名曲，被许多人翻唱。多年后，它以其鼓舞人心的基调和怀着朦胧神性面对即将到来的死亡的悲欣，成为评论

---

[1] [法]马戈汀,古斯登.鲍勃·迪伦的歌：492首歌背后的故事[M].江岭,孙佳慧,等译.郑州：河南大学出版社, 2019.

家和歌迷的至爱。更令人不可思议的是，这首歌被解读为迪伦向美国乃至全世界传递的和平讯息——此时美国正在经受双重打击，一是越南战争失败，一是"水门事件"爆发。这首歌逐渐被赋予反战的内涵，表达止戈为武、刀枪入库的愿景，成为大型集会和体育场音乐会的主打曲目。

除了《比利》，迪伦另一首电影主题曲原本是《再见，霍利》。据迪伦说："菲尔丁一听这歌，突然就发火了。"因此他不得不返工。在墨西哥拍摄电影期间，迪伦灵光一闪突然想到"妈妈，帮我把徽章摘下/我再不可能用到它"这句话。它本是电影中老警长柯林·贝克中枪将死时对妻子的遗言。《敲天堂的门》像流星一样降临了，成了让该片制作人倍感惊喜的电影主题曲。

整张专辑只录制了3场：1973年1月20日在墨西哥1场；2月在洛杉矶附近的伯班克2场。整部电影音乐营造出西部与乡村的气息，苍茫中带有暖意，静谧中含有一丝紧张。在思乡和冥思的旷远气氛中，墨西哥风格的时时渗入，显示着人物故事的地域特征。

迪伦不是专业的电影配乐家，多数时候，他仍是利用自己作为歌手的经验和歌曲创作灵感进行转化。乐思多来自即兴创作，而与美国电影音乐的和声思维及一贯标准着距离。

BILLY

There's guns across the river aimin' at ya
Lawman on your trail, he'd like to catch ya
Bounty hunters, too, they'd like to get ya
Billy, they don't like you to be so free

Campin' out all night on the berenda
Dealin' cards 'til dawn in the hacienda
Up to Boot Hill they'd like to send ya
Billy, don't you turn your back on me

Playin' around with some sweet señorita
Into her dark hallway she will lead ya
In some lonesome shadows she will greet ya
Billy, you're so far away from home

There's eyes behind the mirrors in empty places

比利 [1]

河对岸有枪在对准你
治安官一路追踪,要逮捕你
赏金猎人,也想抓到你
比利,他们不喜欢你自由

在贝伦达 [2] 上整夜露营
在庄园玩牌直到天明
他们想送你上靴子岭 [3]
比利,别转身背对我

与蜜糖小姐逢场作戏
进入她漆黑的走廊时她会带你
置身寂寞的阴影中她会迎你
比利,你离家实在太远

开阔地的镜后有一双双眼

---

[1] 比利小子,美国西部著名枪手,后被警长帕特·加勒特射杀,加勒特曾经是比利的挚友。本篇中出现的地名均在美国新墨西哥州一带,是比利小子出没之处。
[2] 贝伦达,一种针织物。
[3] 靴子岭,美国西部牛仔若死于枪战或绞刑,即被人称为"穿着靴子死",埋葬他们的坟茔人称"靴子岭"。

Bullet holes and scars between the spaces
There's always one more notch and ten more paces
Billy, and you're walkin' all alone

They say that Pat Garrett's got your number
So sleep with one eye open when you slumber
Every little sound just might be thunder
Thunder from the barrel of his gun

Guitars will play your grand finale
Down in some Tularosa alley
Maybe in the Rio Pecos valley
Billy, you're so far away from home

There's always some new stranger sneakin' glances
Some trigger-happy fool willin' to take chances
And some old whore from San Pedro to make advances
Advances on your spirit and your soul

The businessmen from Taos want you to go down
They've hired Pat Garrett to force a showdown
Billy, don't it make ya feel so low-down
To be shot down by the man who was your friend?

两个空旷之间是弹孔和弹痕
总是又多道刻印总是再向前十步 [1]
比利，你总是孤身一人

据说帕特·加勒特掌握了你的秘密
所以睡梦中你也要睁一只眼
每个细小声响都可能是雷霆
雷霆爆出他的枪管

吉他将奏出你的终曲
在图拉罗萨某条小路
也可能是在佩科斯河谷
比利，你离家实在太远

总是有新的陌生人偷瞥你几眼
总是有玩枪的白痴要来冒冒险
圣佩德罗的老婊子总是倒贴你
贴你的神也贴你的魂

陶斯镇的商人巴望着你完蛋
雇了帕特·加勒特逼你摊牌
比利，这岂不让你悲哀
要被你从前的哥们儿开黑枪？

---

[1] 枪手们每杀一人，便在枪柄上刻一道印痕；决斗时，双方各向前走十步，然后拔枪转身射击。

Hang on to your woman if you got one
Remember in El Paso, once, you shot one
She may have been a whore, but she was a hot one
Billy, you been runnin' for so long

Guitars will play your grand finale
Down in some Tularosa alley
Maybe in the Rio Pecos valley
Billy, you're so far away from home

有了个女人就要守住啊
记得在埃尔帕索,有一次,你崩了一个
她也许是个婊子,可是她真惹火
比利,你逃亡实在太久

吉他将奏出你的终曲
在图拉罗萨某条小路
也可能是在佩科斯河谷
比利,你离家实在太远

KNOCKIN' ON HEAVEN'S DOOR

Mama, take this badge off of me
I can't use it anymore
It's gettin' dark, too dark for me to see
I feel like I'm knockin' on heaven's door

Knock, knock, knockin' on heaven's door
Knock, knock, knockin' on heaven's door
Knock, knock, knockin' on heaven's door
Knock, knock, knockin' on heaven's door

Mama, put my guns in the ground
I can't shoot them anymore
That long black cloud is comin' down
I feel like I'm knockin' on heaven's door

Knock, knock, knockin' on heaven's door
Knock, knock, knockin' on heaven's door
Knock, knock, knockin' on heaven's door
Knock, knock, knockin' on heaven's door

敲天堂的门[1]

妈妈,帮我把徽章摘下
我再不可能用到它
天越来越暗,我什么都看不见
我感觉我正在敲天堂的门

敲,敲,敲天堂的门
敲,敲,敲天堂的门
敲,敲,敲天堂的门
敲,敲,敲天堂的门

妈妈,帮我把枪埋到地下
我再不可能使用它
长长的乌云在落下来
我感觉我正在敲天堂的门

敲,敲,敲天堂的门
敲,敲,敲天堂的门
敲,敲,敲天堂的门
敲,敲,敲天堂的门

---

[1] 本篇由郝佳译校。